LIGHTING MARTHA

A One-Act Play About Jean Rosenthal

By Carolyn Gage

The cover art is from Rosenthal's lighting plot for Martha Graham's "Errand into the Maze." The original is at The Rosenthal Collection in the Wisconsin Center for Film and Theater Research. The document can be accessed online at The Lighting Archive. (www.thelightingarchive.org)

Dedicated to Pearl Weinstein

Summary

A One-Act Play

The play opens the night of April 30, 1969, after the final dress rehearsal for Martha Graham's 35th season opener at New York City Center. Legendary lighting designer Jean Rosenthal, dying of cancer, arrived in an ambulance and on a gurney for the final lighting check. She has just left to return to the hospital. Her life partner and lighting assistant, Miki (Marion) Kinsella, is alone on the stage. A lighting technician, Ben, notices her behavior and expresses his concern. Miki is agitated and displacing her anger onto Martha Graham for allowing Jean to attend the rehearsal. Jean has forbidden Miki to talk about her disease or her dying, and Miki's grief and resentment have reached the breaking point. Ben leaves Miki with a pint of whiskey. She turns on the ghost light, lies down on the stage, and falls asleep.

The ghost of a healthy, younger Jean shows up, and Miki challenges her over what she perceives as excessive loyalty to Martha Graham. Jean's explanations only exacerbate Miki's rage, and, in desperation, Jean pulls the plug on the ghost light, retreating into the shadows. In the darkness, the women begin again, and this time, they find a common language—the language of lighting design, for communicating and accepting their difficult truths.

The play is a reflection on denial and dying, intimacy and artists, seeing and being seen, and—of course—on light.

2 women, 40's and 50's; 1 man, 60's
Single set (bare stage)
45 minutes

Introduction

Lighting Martha has traveled a long way from the first draft, written in 2004. The play was originally inspired by a passage in *Staging Desire: Queer Readings of American Theatre History,* where the author described how lighting pioneer Jean Rosenthal, just weeks from dying of cancer, was brought to City Center in an ambulance and on a gurney, in order to supervise the final lighting check for Martha Graham and her dance company's thirty-fifth season.

In researching the first draft, I studied Graham's classic dances in detail, read Graham biographies, researched Rosenthal's life, studied her light plots and her book *The Magic of Light*, and met with Tony-award-winning lighting designer Beverly Emmons, who took me on a tour of City Center. I discovered that Jean's life partner Marion (Miki) Kinsella was still alive, in her 80's, and living on Martha's Vineyard.

I had two phone conversations with Miki. The first one was very promising. I told Miki upfront that I was a playwright who specialized in writing about the lives of famous lesbians, and that I wanted to write a play about Jean Rosenthal, incorporating her lesbianism. When Miki expressed concerns about this, I shared information with her about how Jean's lesbianism and their partnership were already being written about in books and in articles. I told her that this project would provide her with an opportunity to help shape a narrative that was already public. Miki began to open up about networks of lesbians in her and Jean's life. She told me she had photographs that she could show me, and stories she could share. I recognized many of the names from decades of research into lesbian theatre history. We made plans for me to come visit her on the Vineyard.

Several weeks later, I called Miki again, this time to confirm the date and time of the ferry I would be taking. This conversation was so different from the first, it was as if I was speaking to a different person. This Miki was angry and suspicious. She opened by telling me that she had found my website (I had given her the URL), and that she now knew the "kind of work" I did. She appeared not to remember that I had told her about this "kind of work," nor did she remember her invitation to me. She spoke to me as if I was trying to trick her or take advantage of her somehow, dragging her and Jean's name through the mud. And then I heard the clink of ice cubes.

In my career, I encounter homophobia on a weekly basis, and it's often quite virulent. I have lost housing and jobs, and I have been involved in lawsuits because of homophobia. Miki's attack, comparatively minor in terms of material consequences, was still profoundly upsetting to me.

In the end, I did write a draft of a play about Jean Rosenthal, and it was incredibly dull. The play was structured around recreating Jean's lighting design for Martha Graham's "Errand Into the Maze." I had decided to use lighting as a second character. Moss Hart used to say that playwriting was the only profession where one could achieve a level of proficiency and success, and still turn out a project that appeared to have been executed by someone who knew nothing at all about the craft. Such was that draft of *Lighting Martha*.

I put the play away for fourteen years, even as I continued to tell the story of Miki and the ice cubes. Gradually, the pain of that conversation began to recede, and, eventually, I read that Miki had died.

In 2018, I began putting together a second collection of monologues and scenes excerpted from my work. It occurred to me that I might be able to salvage something from my long-abandoned draft of *Lighting Martha*. Working with this material again after so many years, I remembered the hundreds of hours that had gone into the researching of it. Feeling it was a shame to let all that work go to waste, I began to envision a much shorter play that incorporated my experience of Miki, designating her—instead of light!—as the second character.

One of the things that Miki had shared with me in that first conversation was that Jean had arranged for her doctors to have all their consultations with Miki. Jean did not want to know anything about the progression of her cancer or her prognosis. She had left Miki to field all of that information, and Miki was never allowed to talk to Jean about her partner's impending death. When she shared this with me, she expressed a tremendous sense of pain from lack of closure, as well as a lingering resentment.

This dynamic would become the heart of the play. I spent the summer of 2018 studying dying and writing about it in other contexts. I realized that my earlier version of Jean on the gurney was some kind of Disney fantasy. A woman, days from dying of cancer, is not going to be making dramatic speeches that express complex and charged emotions. She cannot possibly take stage in any meaningful way, except as a kind of ghoulish sideshow. In my sixty-seventh year, I was getting real about dying.

The skeletal and heavily medicated Jean has left the building when this version of the play opens. The dialogue is between the angry, grieving, and overwhelmed Miki and the ghost of a younger Jean. The play is about a lesbian who was most comfortable in the shadows, throwing her meticulously designed lighting onto others—the performers. It is especially the story of lighting Martha Graham, the woman who was Jean's first inspiration and perhaps an early crush. It is the story of a life partner who feels she has had to take second place to her lover's all-absorbing career, and who is attempting to confront that before it is too late.

Jean's wisdom about stage lighting guided me in the workshopping of the new draft, which had begun as a play about grieving a lover who was inaccessible. I was directing attention on the emotional shortcomings of a brilliant artist whose life was her work. In production, this perspective appeared shallow and one-sided. I realized that the story—my play—was "poorly lit." And so I went back to what Jean had written about stage lighting. In *The Magic of Light*, she had written:

> *Before the 19th century, lighting's sole purpose was visibility. Then, it gained "theatricality," and began to be used for effects. But in this century, the role of lighting has been refined to aid communication.*

Eureka! "*Refined to aid communication!*" I had been crafting *Lighting Martha* as a kind of searchlight among the shadows of an intimate relationship, seeking out the faults of the one partner in order to cast blame. No wonder it seemed so superficial! The plot was back in the 19th century, focused on visibility and theatricality. In real life, relationships—the interesting ones—are not about villains and victims. Unless train trestles and sawmills are involved, melodramas cannot hold the interest of contemporary theatre audiences.

I rewrote the play with Jean's admonition in mind, repurposing the story to "aid communication"—communication between the two women, and also communication between the play and the audience. I redirected attention on the ways in which both women had benefitted from imbalances in the relationship, and in the process I learned something about life and about myself. If the "scene" of a lifelong relationship is well-lit, assigning blame becomes a moot point. In the words of Emma Goldman, "Before we can forgive one another, we have to understand one another."

Jean's articulation of the higher purpose of lighting illuminated my own craft for me, and *Lighting Martha* became a play that was not about settling scores, but about compassion. It became a play affirming our capacity to heal in our relationships, even after the death of a partner.

Returning to this script, I could see so clearly that I did not have the maturity in my early fifties to take on the subject of dying. Over the last fifteen years, most of my mentors and many of my colleagues have died. I have attended services and written many memorials. My own mortality is no longer an abstraction, but a distinct, ever-present possibility. I have begun the process of putting my house in order, and part of that has included coming to terms with whom and what I have loved, and how I have expressed that love. The primary commitment has always been to the work—to the plays. In *Lighting Martha*, I plead my own case before some imaginary bar, that this love of, and total commitment to the art is also worthy and deserving, a counterweight against manifest deficiencies in relationship histories. In calling for compassion for my characters, I have become a beneficiary myself.

Notes on Jean Rosenthal's Approach to Lighting Design
By Mitchell Jakubka

Jean Rosenthal was not only one of the first lighting designers, and a true trailblazer in her field, but her lighting techniques and status as a lesbian Jewish woman have continued to guide our industry in the decades after her passing. Known for her subtle work with color, and emphasis on crisply sculpted light, she revolutionized the way performance of all genres, and particularly dance, is illuminated. Further, her methods of subverting the blatant sexism and homophobia in the industry have shaped the way lighting designers now work as collaborative artists. She was a master of defeating prejudice with kindness, maintaining an unshakeable calm and giving spirit that endeared her to even her toughest critics. These tactics of personality carried into the work of today's designer, as we strive to maintain gracious, collaborative communication and unending flexibility.

While Jean's personality and lesbian status were major influences on her and our work, her technical prowess was equally important. Across performance media, there are a few key traits that carry through her work and identify something as "a Jean Rosenthal Plot." Generally, each of her systems used a "three color mix," using blendable tones of lavender, a warm, and a cool to mix a variable range of colors and whites. Her cool tones were crisp, pure blue, and slightly more saturated than the other gels in her palette, which helped to combat the fixtures' naturally warm output. Her lavenders and warm tones both tended toward the pinker side of the spectrum, and the lavender was often so pale she referred to it as her "white." The lavender served both to desaturate and blend the other fixtures' color and add sharp intensity. She occasionally used amber tones, but with care, as she believed they could make a scene feel "tired." Though she kept her palettes from straying into super-saturate colors, her mixing system meant that she could sneak in bold color gently (usually in backlight or diagonal backlight), without washing out scenes or performers. She also relied on strong sidelight—particularly from booms, which was a revolution for her time—to shape the performer's bodies and provide a sense of edge and contrast. These bold statements in direction were tempered by the incredible subtlety of her palette and timing. Her cues would fade effortlessly, often using the slowest timing possible, attempting to make the light breathe and flow in a way tied kinetically to the action onstage.

In lighting and performing *Lighting Martha*, one should consider the same aspects that Rosenthal did in her lighting. She was a woman who *felt* light, with each color and angle combination eliciting a different emotional response. Rosenthal may have perceived toplight as repressive, pushing downward, and low sidelight as harsh or upliftingly buoyant, depending on context and color tone. For the climatic final moment of this play, a designer should consider Rosenthal's signature palette—and her physical relation to the angles and colors of light—and pull from this to create a languidly fading display of angle and color combinations that spur the performers to feel a range of emotions.

The difficulty arises when trying to present a tribute to a master's work on a limited stage. In producing *Lighting Martha* in a blackbox theater or other small venue, the designer faces the challenge of creating a wide range of colors, moods, and angles with a small set of lighting tools. To solve these issues, we can again turn back to Rosenthal's original techniques. With her career spanning the early years of lighting design, she too had limited lighting control, and often limited fixture inventories. She solved this issue through careful blending, again using her "three color mix," of warm, cool, and neutral tints. Though modern color changing fixtures may lessen your need to hang many instruments to achieve multiple colors of light, we can follow her example of overlapping a few tones to create a wider range than is possible with just one color per angle. Further, the use of tungsten fixtures allows for the "red shift" of dimming, shifting to a warmer color output of a light as it dims, creating a different tone from the original given at a brighter intensity. This is particularly helpful for the final moment, as we can create multiple colors by choosing to mix (or not mix) multiple fixtures at different angles and intensities, creating many looks from creative use of even the smallest rig. By manipulating blending, brightness, and direction, a designer should be able to create Rosenthal's evocative light in any venue.

Online Resources

http://thelightingarchive.org/show.php?show_id=11#!docID=157
http://www.susanscharfman.com/genius-passion-and-the-magic-of-light.html
https://www.nytimes.com/1996/10/27/arts/lighting-the-way-into-a-sense-of-space.html
http://www3.northern.edu/wild/jr.htm

Mitchell Jakubka is currently a Lighting Design MFA student at Carnegie Mellon University, and a theater and dance lighting designer. His work also spans into queer theater history, and his thesis "A Love of the Whole" examines Jean Rosenthal's historic techniques and her influence on today's lighting designers. MitchellJakubka.com.

Cast of Characters

JEAN ROSENTHAL: The legendary lighting designer, 55. Deeply private.

MIKI KINSELLA: Her partner and assistant, 45. Aggressively devoted to Jean.

BEN: Lighting technician, 60's.

Scene

The stage of New York City Center.

Time

April 30, 1969, late night after the final dress rehearsal for Martha Graham's premiere of *The Archaic Hours.*

Lighting Martha

The darkened stage of New York City Center. It is late at night, April 30, 1969, after the final dress rehearsal for Martha Graham's production, The Archaic Hours. *Everyone has gone home and the theatre is dark. The stage is lit with work lights. There is a single, unlit ghost light to the side. MIKI KINSELLA, 45, stands completely still at center stage, clutching a clipboard and gazing out over the empty theatre. Her life partner is days from dying, and their lesbian relationship cannot be publicly recognized. The partner has forbidden MIKI to talk about her disease or her dying, and MIKI is at a breaking point with repressed grief and rage. BEN, 60, enters. He's a lighting technician. Believing he is alone in the theatre, BEN is humming tunelessly to himself as he crosses upstage of MIKI. He is startled to see her.*

BEN: Miki…? *(Louder.)* Miki? *(She turns.)* I thought you had left… *(MIKI turns wordlessly to look at BEN. He is disconcerted by her silence.)* I thought you left with Jean… *(More silence.)* Are you okay?

MIKI: *(Responding with aggression.)* Sure… Sure, why wouldn't I be?

BEN: *(Smiling.)* The lighting looks great.

MIKI: *(Caustic.)* Of course it does... "Lighting by Jean Rosenthal." The "best on Broadway"… The best in the world! The woman who single-handedly invented the whole field of lighting design. Of course it looks great.

BEN: *(Confused by her aggression.)* Want me to call you a cab…? *(Long silence. He changes tack.)* That was a pretty special dress rehearsal tonight. I don't think anybody on the crew expected to see Jean here.

1

MIKI: *(Her anger building.)* Why not? She told Martha she would light the show. Why wouldn't you expect her for the final dress rehearsal? She's lit every Graham season for the past thirty-four years. Hasn't missed a one.

BEN: Well, Jean is… you know… *(MIKI's not helping him.)* She's pretty sick, isn't she?

MIKI: *"Sick?" (Exploding.)* She's dying, Ben. *Dying.* And *soon.* My partner is dying. *(Turning toward the house, she yells.) Jean Rosenthal is dying! (Turning back to BEN, she smiles.)* I'm not allowed to say that. *Nobody* is allowed to say it, especially her goddam doctors. She makes them all talk to me. She says "Oh, talk to Miki about everything, and then *she* can tell me." And then she says to me, "I don't want to know. I don't want to know *anything.*" It's been like that for the entire last year.

BEN: *(Musing.)* Dying…

MIKI: Dying.

BEN: Well, the crew figured it must be pretty bad, her showing up at City Center tonight in an ambulance…

MIKI: *(Cutting him off.)* Oh, dear God…! The ambulance… and then wheeling her in on a gurney. On a *gurney*! The woman is too damn sick to use a wheelchair, you'd think they'd realize she's too sick to come to work! You'd think they'd have more sense than to let her come at all! You'd think they'd keep her in the goddam hospital! But then *somebody* had the bright idea to bring her on a *gurney*! I don't' know what genius came up with that—

BEN: *(Thoughtfully.)* Could have been Jean…

MIKI: *(Ignoring him.)* And those goddam doctors! Letting her do it! Signing her out! I told them not to, but do they listen to me? Who am I? Just her "lighting assistant?" Her "friend?" Her "roommate?" Why should they listen to me? They all do what Jean says. She always gets her way.

BEN: *(Nodding.)* Oh, yeah. Jeannie gets her way.

MIKI: *(On a tear now.)* Weeks to live…*weeks*! Maybe *days*! And *Martha*! *(She begins to pace.)* I just… I can't even… Martha could have stopped it! She is the only person who could. She's the boss. Martha could have told Jean that she would not allow her in the door at City Center. But did she stop it? No! She *encouraged* her! Standing there, next to that goddam gurney… and Jean—Jean, what—? Weighing seventy pounds and barely able to hold herself up, and Martha's got her bending backwards to check the positions of the lights! I never saw anything so selfish in my life! Like there couldn't be anything more important going on in the universe than lighting Martha Graham. That woman is the most selfish, the most egotistical—

BEN: *(Uncomfortable, he interrupts MIKI's outburst.)* Hey— hey, Miki! Let me call you a cab.

MIKI: No, no… *(Still pacing furiously.)*

BEN: C'mon Miki... It's been a long night.

MIKI: *(Turning on him.)* Where would I go, Ben? Where would I go? Back to the apartment? Her stuff all over the place, and she's never coming home. *She's never coming home!* What am I supposed to do with all that *stuff*… ? *(Her voice has begun to get shaky, but she rallies with anger.)* I don't know what she wants me to do with it, because, God knows, we can't talk about it! Her doctors can't talk about it! Nobody can talk—

BEN: *(Cutting her off.)* Hey! I've got an idea… How about we go somewhere and I buy you a beer?

MIKI: *(She stops pacing and looks at him, suddenly drained.)* No, you go on. You have a show tomorrow.

BEN: So do you.

MIKI. Yeah…

BEN: You know Jeannie's gonna be okay…

MIKI: Ben, she's *dying*.

BEN: Yeah, she is, and she knows it. But she's tough. *(Passing her a flask.)*

MIKI: *(Ignoring the flask.)* I don't know that she's as tough as you think.

BEN: *(Taking a drink himself and then holding it out again.)* How long have you known her?

MIKI: Since 1956. Thirteen years. *(A beat.)* My lucky number. *(She looks at the flask, reconsiders, and takes a swig.)* I worked with her on *West Side Story*.

BEN: *(Nodding)* Yeah?

MIKI: *(Remembering as she takes another drink.)* Cabaret, Hello, Dolly!, Barefoot in the Park… and of course Martha's company… every goddam year… every single goddam—

BEN: Oh, yeah? *(Repossessing the flask.)* I've known Jeannie over thirty years… since the Depression… I met her over at Federal Theatre 891… with Orson Welles. Jeannie was just a kid, but, boy, she stepped right up. Houseman had made her his assistant. And then, when we all lost our jobs for doing that crazy show... the one that got banned... *(Searching his memory.)*

MIKI: *Cradle...*

BEN: Yeah, yeah. *The Cradle Will Rock...* Well, after that, we all went over to the Mercury Theatre with Orson. *(A snort.)* Orson. Ever work with him...?

MIKI: Before my time.

BEN: Oh, yeah. Right. Well, Orson, he always tried to take credit for everything. *(Shaking his head.)* It was Jean who lit *Caesar.* It was Jean who figured out how to do the scene changes without a curtain... the pools of light, the angles ... all Jean. But Orson wouldn't give her the credit ... He called her his "lighting manager, " but I'm telling you, she designed it. She designed the hell out of it. We were all just electricians before Jeannie came along. She was the artist...

MIKI: "Was..."

BEN: *(Still remembering.)* And the guys in the union gave her hell, pure hell... They didn't want to work with a woman and they sure as shootin' weren't going to take orders from one either. They just gave her hell... But she was tough... They'd use the worst language, tell the dirtiest jokes, trying to break her... and they could be kind of rough, too... Shoving her out of the way, knocking her down, acting like they didn't see her. Up in the rigging, too. I remember the day one of the guys didn't like her telling him how to do his job. He said if she did it again, he'd throw his hammer at her. And he did, too. But she stuck it out.

MIKI: I would've had their asses fired so fast... *(She takes the flask back and takes another swig.)*

5

BEN: You couldn't… not thirty years ago. Jeannie just had to ride it out. But she never let them see she was mad. She never raised her voice. And the more they disrespected her, the more she went out of her way to treat them with courtesy. You know she was always real careful not to embarrass us. If there was somebody doing something the wrong way… she'd just take the guy over to the side, like she was having some kind of professional consult with him… and that's when she'd tell him. Making sure nobody else could hear what she was saying. That made an impression. You bet it did. Oh, yeah.

MIKI: Saint Rosenthal. *(A toast.)* Our Lady of the Lights.

BEN: You know how, when she comes through the door, you hear someone yell out, "Jean's in the house…?"

MIKI: Yeah…

BEN: Well, that's so the boys all know to clean up their language. Some new guy starts mouthing off in front of her, we straighten him out real fast.

MIKI: But, Ben, you let her come here tonight on a gurney. On a fucking *hospital gurney*!

BEN: Miki, she wanted it that way… *(MIKI, turns away, fighting back tears. Long pause.)* C'mon… let me get you a cab…

MIKI: No. I'm okay. *(Handing back the flask without turning.)* You go on home.

BEN: It's not good to be by yourself.

MIKI: There's worse things than being alone, trust me…. Don't worry about me. Hey, I even got me a ghost light. *(She crosses*

6

over to the ghost light, still hiding her face from him. She switches it on.) I bet the dead are a hell of a lot more fun than the dying.

BEN: You sure? *(No response.)* Okay. *(He starts to leave, halts, and then sets the flask on the floor as he exits. On the way out BEN throws the breakers. There is a loud clang as the stage goes dark except for the illumination from the ghost light.)*

MIKI: *(Turning to see if he's gone, MIKI notices the flask, and retrieves it. She addresses the empty theatre.)* Well, come on, all you theatre ghosts… Don't mind me… Just pretend I'm not here. That's what I intend to do. *(Stretching out on the stage, she falls asleep. JEAN ROSENTHAL enters. This is Jean from 1967, before the cancer. She's in her mid-fifties and in good health. She walks up to the ghost light, holding her hands, palms outward, as if she was warming them in a fire. JEAN, who experiences light as tactile, caresses the edges of the light. She looks toward the sleeping MIKI, smiles and crosses down to her. Sitting cross-legged on the floor, she looks at MIKI. Slowly MIKI opens her eyes. She is momentarily confused.)* Jean…? *(JEAN waves a hand.)* This is a dream. *(JEAN smiles.)* Yeah, this is definitely a dream… You're not dying. You're not skinny enough. The real Jean is back at the hospital. *(She rolls over, turning her back on JEAN.)*

JEAN: "The real Jean…?"

MIKI: Yeah. *(Pause.)* The nightmare Jean. The Jean that isn't even Jean anymore. But she is.

JEAN: I know. I see her, too.

MIKI: *(MIKI rolls back to look at JEAN. She studies her for a moment.)* What are you? *(JEAN smiles and points toward the ghost light.)* Ah. The ghost light… *(Sitting upright.)* Wait! Is Jean… is she… ?

7

JEAN: No... No, she's still alive.

MIKI: But you're her ghost...?

JEAN: Well... More the form of her spirit.

MIKI: Doesn't that mean...?

JEAN: Sometimes, if there is something that needs to be taken care of... something urgent—the spirit can appear before the actual death.

MIKI: What is it? *(Uncomfortable, JEAN crosses away from MIKI to the front of the stage, looking at the lighting.)* Tell me why you're here!

JEAN: *(Referring to the lights.)* We did a nice job, didn't we?

MIKI: We? *I* did most of the work. You were too sick. Tell me what this thing is... this thing that's so urgent a ghost has come calling.

JEAN: Spirit. *(A beat.)* Miki... I'm going to need a little time.

MIKI: You don't have any. You'd know that if you talked to your doctors.

JEAN: *(Looking at the lights again.)* They look really good.

MIKI: *(Angry.)* I wish to hell I hadn't agreed to do it!

JEAN: Why?

MIKI: *(Rising and really beginning to engage.)* Because you wouldn't have taken the job without me, and it was too much! *(Shaking her head.)* It was too goddam much...

8

JEAN: But I promised Martha. I couldn't let her down.

MIKI: You couldn't let her down? Why not? Why the hell not? You don't owe that woman a thing! She owes *you*! Thirty-five years of lighting her shows. She should have come to the hospital tonight, instead of you and that damn ambulance coming to City Center… *(Pacing.)* Thirty-five years is not enough, but that vampire has to drain your last ounce of lifeblood, your last… your last… *(MIKI is so angry she can't find words.)* …*everything*! *(She stops and confronts JEAN.)* You don't owe Martha Graham a goddam thing!

JEAN: *(Quietly)* Miki… I do.

MIKI: No! I don't want to hear it. Not after tonight… Not after this… this… ghoulish pageant… ambulance, gurney, a Greek chorus of orderlies and nurses… everything but the professional mourners… Oh, I guess that was *me*, because it certainly wasn't Martha! *She's* got a show to do! God forbid your decaying body should get in the way of *her* dress rehearsal. *(JEAN looks away.)* *What*? What the hell could you possibly owe that woman?

JEAN: Being "Jean Rosenthal."

MIKI: More like she owes you for making her "Martha Graham."

JEAN: Miki, she—

MIKI: *(Holding up her hand.)* No! I don't want to hear it!

JEAN: All right… *(Long pause.)* …But—

MIKI: No! *(A beat.)* No… *(Long pause.)*

JEAN: Just one thing—

MIKI: I said I don't want to hear it! Not after tonight... *(Long, long silence. JEAN turns to leave. MIKI capitulates.)* Okay. But just one thing.

JEAN: I danced with her.

MIKI: You did not.

JEAN: She said I had peasant feet.

MIKI: No.

JEAN: It was a compliment.

MIKI: I don't believe you. *(JEAN looks at her.)* When?

JEAN: Before you were born.

MIKI: *(Annoyed.) When?*

JEAN: 1929.

MIKI: *(Defensively.)* I was five years old. *(JEAN smiles. Long silence.)* All right. Why were you dancing with Martha Graham?

JEAN: Because I couldn't get into college. None of them would have me, because of all the experimental schools I had gone to. So my parents sent me to the Neighborhood Playhouse School. They thought it might broaden my horizons. *(JEAN smiles.)*

MIKI: And you signed up for Martha's dance class...

JEAN: I didn't have a choice! They made me! They made everybody take everything! That's how the Playhouse was... The set designers had to study dance, and the dancers had to study voice, and they made all the actors learn musical composition. It was crazy… You should have seen us—

MIKI: *(Suddenly overwhelmed, she reaches for her.)* Jean… I miss you—

JEAN: *(Quickly moving away.)* Don't!

MIKI: Why?

JEAN: It's a spirit thing… You can't touch me.

MIKI: Oh. "A ghost thing…" *(MIKI crosses away. JEAN watches her with compassion. MIKI turns, angry.)* What are you doing here? What the hell are you doing here?

JEAN: *(Long silence.)* Really, Miki… you should have seen us… There we were, all us teenaged girls… with our chic, little, bobbed haircuts and our shapeless, little sack-dresses… thinking we were the cat's pajamas… so worldly and so sophisticated… and then…

MIKI: Yeah. "Then Martha."

JEAN: *(Turning to look at her. MIKI does not take her eyes off JEAN during this speech.)* She threw open that classroom door and just stood there… that long black hair halfway down her back, and this… this robe…! Yards and yards of fabric… She had made it herself. It didn't look like anything that anyone was wearing in 1929. She was like some kind of priestess from another dimension. You know what it was? She was *feral*. That's what it was. She had not been domesticated. She was standing outside of everything that we thought mattered. And suddenly it was as if all of us girls were just little paper dolls lying flat in a box, waiting for someone to pick us up and play with us. Imagine meeting Martha Graham when you were young!

MIKI: *(Attempting to redirect the conversation.)* I met *you* when I was young.

JEAN: *(Lost in the memory.)* She told us that we were not here to please the audience. *(She turns to MIKI.)* Imagine a young girl hearing those words forty years ago… "We are not here to please the audience." She said that ugliness, if it had a powerful voice, was beautiful. Strength was the thing. She was so incredibly strong.

MIKI: *You're* the strongest woman I ever met.

JEAN: I remember that first day so clearly. She told us to take off our shoes and lie down on our backs. All twenty of us girls… lying on the floor. And then suddenly, she shouted "Contract!" And we all contracted. And then she shouted "Release!"… and we all released. "Contract!" "Release!" "Contract!" "Release!" Over and over… And while we're doing this, Martha delivers a sermon about how all movement begins in the "house of pelvic truth."

MIKI: *(Shaking her head.)* "The house of pelvic truth…"

JEAN: *(Playfully intimate.)* Well, I thought I had died and gone to heaven.

MIKI: No doubt.

JEAN: There's no going back from that house of pelvic truth.

MIKI: *(Ruefully.)* Don't I know it. *(MIKI reaches for JEAN's hand, but JEAN pulls it away. MIKI watches her.)* So you had a crush on Teacher.

JEAN: Huge. I fell down a flight of stairs for her.

MIKI: Pretty serious.

12

JEAN: I accidentally-on-purpose injured my back so I couldn't dance anymore and Martha would have to take me on as her technical assistant.

MIKI: Clever.

JEAN: It was my job to get her whatever she needed. And one day the "thing" that Martha needed was light. *(JEAN is overwhelmed with wonder by the memory.)*

MIKI: *(Turning away suddenly.)* I don't want to talk about her anymore. *(JEAN lowers her head and looks at her hands.)* What about *us*... *You*? Jean, you're *dying*, but you won't let us talk about it, and now it's too late. You're drugged and sleeping all the time. There's nothing but pain. There's nothing left to say. *(JEAN doesn't say anything.) You're leaving me!* Do you even love me?

JEAN: *(Protesting.)* Of course.

MIKI: What do you mean, "of course?"

JEAN: *(Pleading.)* We live together. You're my assistant... We've been working together for—

MIKI: *Exactly*! Your *assistant*! I'm your *assistant*! And how handy to live with your *assistant*! Just like Nan Porcher before me... Why, it's like having your own personal employee seven days a week, twenty-four hours a day...!

JEAN: Miki—

MIKI: No, I'm serious.

JEAN: We're lovers!

MIKI: Maybe that's just part of the job description.

JEAN: Don't be cruel, Miki.

MIKI: Me? Me "don't be cruel?" How about you making all the doctors talk to me? *I'm* the one who has to hear about the tumors and the blood tests, and where it's metastasized to, and how sick the radiation is going to make you, and how long you have to live. You don't want to hear any of it, so you make me hear it.

JEAN: Stop, Miki!

MIKI: You want to know how long you have to live?

JEAN: No! Stop it! *(Covering her ears.)*

MIKI: *(Pursuing her.)* You want to know?

JEAN: Stop! Stop!

MIKI: Two weeks. *(Raising her voice.)* *Two weeks*! *(JEAN has retreated. For MIKI, a dam has broken.)* I'm *not* sorry! I'm sorry I didn't say it sooner! Jean, we've been living a goddam lie... Pretending I'm your roommate, pretending I'm just your assistant... pretending you don't have cancer, pretending you're not dying! *(She looks at JEAN defensively.)* I don't care! You know what it's like? It's like the time you were hired to light the tour of those Russian ballet dancers... Nijinsky's sister... remember? You told me her choreography was all in the first ten feet of the stage, because all they had in their theatres were gas footlights. *(Indicating their locations.)* So that's what they asked for... just to light those first ten feet... *(Indicating the positions of these lights.)* First pipe and two booms...That's what they wanted. But you... *you* needed to light behind them and around them and above them, because that's what Martha had taught you... that every area of the stage was important... that wherever she was dancing, *that* was center stage. But what would be the

14

point of that with these Russian dancers, because they *couldn't* dance where you wanted to light them? And in the end, they threw you out. And now you've lit just this narrow, little strip of your life—what's left of it—and you've made both of us dance in that strip. Jean, you are dying! You are leaving! There is so much space—*so much space*—behind us and around us and above us, and *we can't move in it*! This flat little dance of denial right out in front of everybody… that's all you want to light! I can't do it anymore! I have things to say and do that are all over the place! All over the place, Jean! I can't do the goddam footlights dance anymore, and you won't move the booms for me!

JEAN: *(Anguished.)* I *can't* move the booms.

MIKI: You always say, "Your lighting will expose you." Well, it has. You don't love me. *You don't love me.* You never loved me. All you love is the work… the work and *Martha*!

JEAN: Miki, please…

MIKI: What? Do you want to run over the light cues again? After all, what could be more important than lighting Martha? *(She grabs her clipboard.)* Which cues did you want to look at, Miss Rosenthal?

JEAN: No, Miki…

MIKI: Not the cues? How about the lighting positions then? Where should we start…?

JEAN: Please…

MIKI: Oh, let's start here… The first pipe… Those precious first ten feet… that's what really counts. That's what's important—

JEAN: *(In agony.)* No! Stop it...! *(The ghost light suddenly cuts out, plunging the stage into near-total darkness. JEAN retreats to the shadows. A long silence.)*

MIKI: Jean...? Jean...? *(Long silence.)* Shit. *(She shouts into the theatre.)* I'm sorry! I'm sorry, I'm sorry, I'm sorry...! It's been a long night... an *endless* night! It's been the worst night of my fucking life...! And I know you came here to tell me something—or to do something—important... and I just... I'm sorry... Please come back.

JEAN: *(Stepping out from the shadows.)* I never left.

MIKI: *(Quickly.)* I'll get the light... *(MIKI starts to cross to the ghost light.)*

JEAN: *No, don't! (MIKI turns.)* Leave it off... please.

MIKI: But I thought ghosts—

JEAN: I like the dark. It reminds me of the light booth.

MIKI: Ah. *(A beat.)* The light booth... Oh, my god, Jean... How many hours, days... how many *years* of our lives have we spent together in a lightbooth?

JEAN: Why don't we imagine that we're in one now? *(She crosses next to MIKI.)*

MIKI: *(She looks at JEAN. Long silence. Nodding, MIKI turns to face the empty theatre.)* Okay. We're in a lightbooth together. So... what's the play?

JEAN: Well, it's about two women. They've been together for a long time. One of them is very sick and in this scene, she is lying on a bed.

16

MIKI: Or a gurney…

JEAN: The other woman is her partner—

MIKI: Her assistant.

JEAN: *(Reproving her gently.)* Miki…

MIKI: Okay… Two women… *Partners…*

JEAN: And they really need to talk, but they can't really see each other.

MIKI: Why not?

JEAN: Because the scene hasn't been properly lit.

MIKI: And whose fault is that? *(A beat.)* Sorry. *(Pause. MIKI adopts a professional attitude.)* Okay. So… two women, one in the bed, the other not… Why can't we just bring up the front light on the bed?

JEAN: Well… that's going to be a problem, because the woman—the one who is sick—doesn't want to be seen.

MIKI: Why not?

JEAN: Well… If she answers that question, she's going to be seen.

MIKI: *(A long pause. MIKI is starting to understand.)* Yeah. That's a problem. That's a *real* problem. *(JEAN nods.)* But what about backlighting? If we backlit her, that wouldn't put a light directly on her, but we could still make out her profile.

JEAN: *(Considering.)* That could work…

MIKI: Okay... backlighting, then? *(JEAN nods.)* The woman who is sick... her family were immigrants, weren't they?

JEAN: *(She takes a deep breath.)* Yes. Both her father and her mother came over from Romania with their families. They were both children... poor, not speaking English. And they had to work very hard. They worked all the time. It's who they were...

MIKI: *(Gazing at the imaginary scene.)* Okay. This is helping...

JEAN: *(Nodding, she resumes.)* Well... the father became an ear, nose and throat doctor, and the mother became a psychiatrist. And then they had children... two boys and a girl. And the parents and the boys... Well, they were all just incredibly strong-willed... And so the little girl learned that it was easier just to get out of their way... to stay in the shadows, to make herself invisible...

MIKI: *I* see you, Jean.

JEAN: *(A beat.)* And one of the schools they sent her to was out in the country... on a farm. It was kind of a socialist experiment. Everyone had to sleep in tents... and every morning somebody had to go to the henhouse and get the eggs for breakfast. And that could be pretty scary, so the girl learned how to get those eggs without disturbing the chickens... And that's how she survived the stage workers' union.

MIKI: People aren't chickens.

JEAN: But it was the same. The stagehands sat on their precious union jobs, just like hens guarding their eggs. They didn't want women coming in and "stealing" them... Miki, this is who I am. Working behind the scene, in the shadows. And when I got sick, I didn't want the doctors all studying me like I was a specimen— putting a spotlight on my body. It was unbearable! That's why I asked them to talk to you! I didn't mean to hurt you… I thought you would understand…

MIKI: *(Stricken.)* But I didn't… Oh, my god, I didn't get that at at all… Shit—

JEAN: Well, how could you? The woman in the bed doesn't want to be seen.

MIKI: *(Becoming agitated.)* No! No, look again! That's *not* the problem…! It's *not* the woman in bed. It's the other one! It's the *other one* who is the problem! *(She grabs the ghost light and turns it on, holding it very close to her face. The effect is alarming.)* It's the assistant—!

JEAN: Miki…

MIKI: No, look at her! She's the one who has been hiding! Hiding in plain sight. That's her strategy! Everyone thinking she's so devoted, so selfless… such a *martyr* to her famous partner! But *look at her*! She's an assistant because she doesn't want the responsibility! She doesn't want the responsibility for designing the lights… or designing her life! She's a coward! A passive-aggressive, little coward who blames her brilliant, wonderful partner for everything in her life that isn't working!

JEAN: Oh, no, Miki, that's too harsh! Turn it off!

MIKI: A selfish coward!

JEAN: Oh, for heaven's sake—It isn't a melodrama! *(She reaches over and turns off the light.)* There are no villains or victims here. It's just an improperly lit scene. A glare is no better than the shadows, because it's *not about visibility* and it's not about melodrama, either. That was another century, but today, the whole purpose of stage lighting is to *aid communication*.

19

That's what we're doing here… That's why I'm here. *(MIKI starts to protest.)* Listen to me, Miki… When I started working for Martha as her assistant, nobody—*nobody*—took her seriously. Nobody could see what she was doing in dance. They made fun of her… She wasn't pretty. She was too old. Her movements weren't graceful. That's what they saw. And Martha was in so much pain, because she was giving so much, and nobody could see it! And I was just aching to let her know that *I* saw her, and that *I* saw what she was doing and how important it was. Miki, I loved her so much I thought I would explode. And then she asked me to light her, and even though I was back in the shadows, I was able to take that love and just pour it all over her! I covered her with light; I caressed her with light… I tickled her and I teased her with light! I studied Martha so intimately, I could anticipate her movements, so that the light would be there just a split second before she needed it. And, Miki, she *received* it. She danced *with* my light, not just *in* it. I remember she told me she wanted this long, diagonal light that would start from the back of the stage and cross down to the front… And I designed it for her. She named it "the Finger of God," and Martha flirted with my Finger of God. At first, she would avoid it. She would work around it. And then she built it into the dance, into her character. My lighting became part of her struggle and search… and always, always, after approaching it and avoiding it… edging toward it, edging away… always, by the end of the dance, she would land right in the heart of it. You call this my work, but it's love. Miki, this *is* love to me, and when I asked you to be my assistant I thought I was sharing with you the greatest gift in the world.

MIKI: *(Stricken with guilt.)* I didn't deserve it.

JEAN: Miki—

MIKI: It's late… I should go. I have another ghost, tonight… in the hospital…

JEAN: Wait… *(A small light comes up on MIKI. MIKI turns to face it.)*

MIKI: What? *(Another light comes up on her, and then another. MIKI freezes.)*

JEAN: Can you feel it? *(More lights, shifting and changing.)* Can you feel the light?

MIKI: *(With a laugh.)* Jean, you are literally the only person on this whole planet who can feel light. *(A beat, as more lights shift and appear.)* Come here… Please. *(A pause.)* I'm not Martha. I don't want to be alone in the light. I need to share it with you. *(Slowly, JEAN steps out from the shadows and into the light with MIKI. More colors, more intensity, more movement. JEAN, facing the light, holds out her hands and closes her eyes, touching the light ecstatically. MIKI watches her from behind, overwhelmed.)*

JEAN: You really can't you feel this?

MIKI: *(Eyes only for JEAN.)* Yes. I believe I can. *(JEAN turns to look at her.)* I really can. Jeannie, it's beautiful. *(JEAN smiles and turns back to face the light. MIKI is suddenly overwhelmed with emotion.)* Oh, my god, I love you so much! *(She reaches her arms around JEAN to clasp her from behind. The stage is plunged into darkness.)* Jean…? Jean? *(MIKI crosses in the dark to the ghost light and switches it on. She glances around the stage, understanding that JEAN is gone. Turning to face the empty theatre, she looks up toward the lights, nodding with the relief of acceptance.)* "Lighting by Jean Rosenthal." *(She exits.)*

Blackout

End of Play

Play Collections and Drama Books

By Carolyn Gage

The Second Coming of Joan of Arc and Selected Plays

Nine Short Plays

Black Eye and Other Short Plays

Three Comedies

The Triple Goddess: Three Plays

Starting from Zero: One-Act Plays about Lesbians in Love

The Very Short Plays

Monologues and Scenes for Lesbian Actors

More Monologues and Scenes for Lesbian Actors

Take Stage: How To Direct and Produce a Lesbian Play

What Others Are Saying

"… Carolyn Gage is one of the best lesbian playwrights in America…"--*Lambda Book Report,* **Los Angeles.**

"…The culture of women we have never had is invented in Carolyn Gage's brilliant and beautiful plays."—**Andrea Dworkin, feminist philosopher activist, and author.**

"The work of an experienced and esteemed playwright like Carolyn Gage is the air that modern theatre needs.—**Jewelle Gomez, author of *The Gilda Stories,* San Francisco Arts Commissioner.**

"Carolyn Gage is a fabulous feminist playwright, and a major one too. This is great theatre. Gage's dramatic and lesbian imagination is utterly original… daring, heartbreaking, principled, bitter, and often very funny… There is no rhetoric here: only one swift and pleasurable intake of breath after another… Women's mental health would improve, instantly, were they able to read and see these plays performed."— **Phyllis Chesler, author of *Women and Madness.***

"… the toughest, most lesbian/feminist-identified work for theatre I know… brilliant and daring scripts…"— **John Stoltenberg, former Executive Editor, *On the Issues*, author of *Refusing to Become A Man.***

"No playwright has created as amazing a pantheon of historical lesbian characters as Carolyn Gage. Her book, *Monologues and Scenes for Lesbian Actors*, provides a sumptuous feast of possibilities for both seasoned and budding lesbian performers to use portraying a full range of emotion and political perspectives. Carolyn Gage is a national lesbian treasure."—**Rosemary Keefe Curb, editor of *Amazon All Stars : 13 Lesbian Plays.***

"*Mahalo nui* for your play. It is splendid, *clever*, and sets the characters in an imaginary world that is,nevertheless, quite believable. The mark of superb craftsmanship...! *Ku'e, ku'e,ku'e!* [Resist, resist, resist!]"— **Haunani-Kay Trask, leader of the Hawai'ian Sovereignty Movement.**

"Carolyn Gage's writing, acting, and teaching are explosive. She rips away the cultural camouflage that permits us to accept, to be blind to, the brutal context in which women are still required to live their lives. When my students remember this semester it will be because of her visit. She's a treasure."— **Prof. George Wolf, Dept. of English, University of Nebraska, Lincoln.**

"Carolyn Gage is a living manifestation of the power of articulate anger. Her play is raw, uncompromising, in your face, and her politics are no different. In the flesh, however, her passion, humour and quicksilver insight shine through her rage against the patriarchal machine. An inspired spokeswoman for revolutionary radical feminism, I love to think of Carolyn out there now, urging women all over the world to access that submerged anger that, once released, will enable them to find hope, pleasure, selfhood."—*Women's News*, **Belfast, Northern Ireland**

"... The undisputed queen of startling one-acts."—**Victoria K. Brownworth, Pulitzer Prize nominee, author of *Too Queer*.**

Carolyn Gage

Carolyn Gage is a lesbian feminist playwright, performer, director, and activist. The author of seventy-five plays and eight collections of plays, she specializes in non-traditional roles for women, especially those reclaiming famous lesbians whose stories have been distorted or erased from history. In 2019, her play *The Second Coming of Joan of Arc* opens Off-Broadway.

In 2014, she was one of the six featured playwrights at the 53rd Annual World Theatre Day, sponsored by UNESCO, and held in Rome. In 2014 she also received a Lifetime Achievement Award from Venus Theatre in Laurel, Maryland. In 2015, the Sophia Smith Collection at Smith College acquired her papers.

In 2011, her *Stigmata* won the Maine Literary Award in Drama from the Maine Writers and Publishers Alliance. Also in 2011, her play *The Ladies' Room* was named national finalist for the prestigious Heideman Award, given to the winner of the National 10-Minute Play Contest of the Actors' Theatre of Louisville. Her collection of plays *The Second Coming of Joan of Arc and Selected Plays* won the 2008 Lambda Literary Award in Drama, the top LGBT book award in the US. In 2009, she was named one of the "Ten Most Intriguing People in Maine" by *Portland Magazine*, and was awarded a three-month residency at the Wurlitzer Foundation in Taos, New Mexico. In 2010, she was named one of the "Most Influential People in Portland" by the *Portland Phoenix.*

For more than two decades, Gage toured internationally in her award-winning, one-woman play, *The Second Coming of Joan of Arc*, offering performances, workshops, and lectures on lesbian theatre. In 2008, her new musical about Babe Didrikson was given concert readings in both Phoenix and Minneapolis, and her play *The Countess and the Lesbians* premiered at the Dublin International Gay Theatre Festival, where it was reviewed by *The Irish Times* and sold out the run. In 2009, a revised and expanded version of her collection of *Monologues and Scenes for Lesbian Actors* was published, along with her anthology *The Spindle and Other Lesbian Fairy Tales.*

In 2004, her play *Ugly Ducklings* was nominated by the American Theatre Critics Association for the prestigious ATCA/ Steinberg New Play Award, an award with given annually for the best new play produced outside New York. It won the Lesbian Theatre Award from *Curve Magazine*, and a $150,000 documentary on the play premiered at the Frameline International Film Festival in San Francisco. *The Anastasia Trials in the Court of Women* was named National Finalist for the Jane Chambers Award given by the Association for Theatre in Higher Education. Receiving top reviews in Miami and in Washington, DC, it was the subject of a feature article in *The Washington Post.* Her one act, *Harriet Tubman Visits a Therapist*, was presented at Actors Theatre of Louisville in the Juneteenth Festival of African American plays. It was a national winner of the Samuel French Off-Off Broadway Festival, and is included in Random House's anthology *Under 30: Plays for a New Generation.*

Gage's musical, *The Amazon All Stars* is the first lesbian full book musical ever published by a mainstream play publisher. Published by Applause Books, it is the title work of an anthology of lesbian plays that was a national finalist for the Lambda Literary Award. Her manual on lesbian theatre production, *Take Stage! How to Direct and Produce a Lesbian Play* was published by Scarecrow Press.

Gage's work has been endorsed by feminist authors and activists, including Andrea Dworkin, Mary Daly, Phyllis Chesler, Victoria A. Brownworth, Diana E.H. Russell, and John Stoltenberg. Gage was named contributing editor to the national feminist quarterly *On the Issues.* Her essays and short stories have been published in the *Dramatists Guild Quarterly, Trivia, Sinister Wisdom, Lesbian Ethics, The Lesbian Review of Books, The Gay and*

Lesbian Review, The Michigan Quarterly Review, The Lambda Book Report, and *off our backs.* Gage has written the first meditation book for feminist activists, *Like There's No Tomorrow: Meditations for Women Leaving Patriarchy.*

In 2008, Gage lectured at Tisch School of the Arts at New York University, and she was appointed Guest Lecturer at Bates College in Maine. She has won the Oregon Playwrights Award from the Oregon Institute of Literary Arts as well as the Maine Playwrights Award from the Maine Writers and Publishers Alliance. She has also been awarded grants from the Maine Arts Commission, the Maine Women Writers' Collection at the University of New England, the Walden Writer's Fellowship from Lewis and Clark College, the Oregon Institute of Literary Arts Writer's Grant, and the Oregon Arts Commission Individual Artist Grant. In 2005, she won the national Lynda Hart Memorial Grant from the Astraea Foundation. Gage has also received the Janine C. Rae Award for the Advancement of Women's Culture from the National Women's Music Festival. Former recipients include Audre Lorde, June Jordan, Margarethe Cammermeyer, Nikki Giovanni, Del Martin and Phyllis Lyon.

One of the most prolific feminist playwrights in the world, Carolyn Gage is a dynamic speaker and a powerful role model.

www.ingramcontent.com/pod-product-compliance
Lightning Source LLC
Chambersburg PA
CBHW061231280526
45784CB00006B/2724